"Rhina P. Espaillat's translations of the verse of San Juan de la Cruz are a marvel of poetic re-creation. Her celebrated skill as a formalist poet in English, together with her native fluency in Spanish and her deep understanding of his work, gives readers in the Anglophone world all the beauty and mystical vision of his poems. Indeed, Espaillat's translations show us why San Juan de la Cruz is recognized as one of the greatest poets in Spanish literature."

—JONATHAN COHEN, author of *A Pan-American Life*

"At last we have this book of mystical poems by the Spanish saint, San Juan de la Cruz. Translator Rhina P. Espaillat has accurately and lushly rendered his paradoxes and rhapsodies using rhymes, meters, and rhythms that closely echo the music of the original Spanish. Enjoy it for yourself, then give copies to friends who love the work of John Donne and Gerard Manley Hopkins."

—A.M. JUSTER

The Spring that Feeds the Torrent

Copyright © 2023 by Wiseblood Books

All rights reserved, including the right to reproduce this book or any portions thereof in any form whatsoever except for brief quotations in book reviews. For information, address the publisher:

> Wiseblood Books
> P.O. Box 870
> Menomonee Falls, WI 53052

Printed in the United States of America

Set in Baskerville URW Typesetting

Cover design by Amanda Brown

Cover art from retablo by Lynn Garlick

ISBN 13: 978-1-951319-09-0

The Spring that Feeds the Torrent

Poems by Saint John of the Cross

La fonte que mana y corre

versos de San Juan de la Cruz

Translated by Rhina P. Espaillat

Wiseblood Books

This bilingual sampling of the work of San Juan de la Cruz is dedicated, with my gratitude and admiration, to the excellent Dominican poet Juan Matos, who has worked tirelessly, through his founding and leadership of "Miercoletras," to introduce poets of the Americas to each other, across both geographic borders and language boundaries.

Contents

Introduction by Timothy Murphy

1

A Word from the Translator
about St. John of the Cross

7

Cántico espiritual

12

A Spiritual Canticle of the
Soul and the Bridegroom Christ

13

Glosa: Sin arrimo y con arrimo

34

Glosa: Apart and Not Yet a Part

35

Glosa a lo divino

38

Glosa to the Divine

39

Entréme donde no supe: Coplas

48

I Went In, I Knew Not Where

49

Letrillos
1. Navidad
2. Suma de la perfección

54

Quatrains
1. Nativity
2. The Sum of Perfection

55

*Cantar de la alma que se huelga
de conoscer a Dios por fee*

56

Song of the Soul that Takes Pleasure
in Knowing God by Faith

57

*Canciones de el alma en la íntima
comunicación de unión de amor de Díos*

62

Songs of the Soul in Intimate
Amorous Communion with God

63

Coplas: Tras de un amoroso lance

66

Coplas: In Pursuit

67

El pastorcico

70

The Youthful Shepherd

71

Coplas del alma que pena por ver a Dios

74

Verses of the Soul that Pines to See God

75

*En una noche oscura:
Cançión de la subida del Monte Carmel*

80

The Dark Night of the Soul

81

Acknowledgments
85

About St. John of the Cross
89

About the Translator
91

Introduction

"Translations are like lovers: There are those that are beautiful but untrue and those that are true but unbeautiful."

An old saw, perhaps, but I first heard it from the poet Dick Davis, himself a talented translator from medieval Persian. Nonetheless, we live in a glorious age for poetic translation, beginning with the work of Richard Wilbur. Dana Gioia, whose own *Hercules Furens* is one of the best englishings we have of classical tragedy, once suggested that Wilbur's translations are so good, he ought to collect them for his fellow poets in a single volume, to be titled *Look on My Works, Ye Mighty, and Despair.*

In his remarkable Sappho to Valery, the late John Frederick Nims translates from Latin and Greek, Italian and Spanish, French and German and Galician, Catalan, and Provençal, for heaven's sake. In his preface to the book, Nims asserts: "One cannot translate a poem, but one can try to reconstitute it by taking the thought, the imagery, the rhythm, the sound, the qualities of diction, these and whatever else made up the original, and then attempt to rework as many as possible into a poem in English." He continues, "with poetry, to translate the thought alone is not enough; indeed, it is next to nothing. If the translator is trying to show us how the poetry goes, what he writes has to be first of all a poem."

Some of the most remarkable translations which I've encountered in recent years are Rhina Espaillat's translations of St. John of the Cross.

As it happens, Espaillat is celebrated for translations in the other direction, notably her renderings of Robert Frost into Spanish. I have about enough Spanish to order a *cerveza fria*, but I laughed with delight when I saw her effortlessly duplicate the demanding rhyme scheme of "Stopping by Woods on a Snowy Evening." Frost, who famously defined poetry as "that which is lost in translation," would have been similarly delighted.

These translations of St. John, however, show her skill at moving from Spanish to English. Nims' masterful *Poems of St. John of the Cross* first appeared in 1959, and he spent half his very long life revising the texts. But Espaillat's translations strike me as less effortful and more contemporary, and I suspect they are nearer the original. St. John was her father's favorite poet, she has had him in memory from early childhood, and her Spanish rivals her mastery of English. Poetic translation, requiring as it does adherence not just to beauty but to truth, is far more difficult an art than the composition of original verse. Espaillat's translations of these very substantial poems are coming so fluently that one wonders whether the Holy Spirit is not directing her pen in some sort of private Pentecost.

Unlike most poets, St. John brings sinners to Christ. My confessor gave up his life as a drug-dealing saloon keeper when he heard Loreena McKennitt sing her musically ravishing but textually challenged version of "En Una Noche Oscura." I recited him Rhina's translation, which concludes:

> *I stayed, all else forgetting,*
> *inclined toward the beloved, face to face;*
> *all motion halted, letting*
> *care vanish with no trace,*
> *forgotten in the lilies of that place.*

The young priest smiled broadly: "So that's what he said!" One difficulty for any translator of St. John is that his expressed passion for his Redeemer surpasses the merely sensual and reaches, like Song of Songs, into the explicitly sexual:

O night that led me true,
O night more fair than morning's earliest shining,
O night that wrought from two,
lover, beloved entwining,
beloved and lover one in their combining!
On my new-flowered breast,
to him alone and wholly sanctified,
he leaned and lay at rest;
his pleasure was my guide,
and cedars to the wind their scent supplied.

No other great poet of the personal relation to Christ—not Gerard Manley Hopkins, not George Herbert—takes us so far into the bower of Christ and his poet bride. Other than St. John, who but a passionate woman could do so? Consider "The Youthful Shepherd," which opens, in Rhina's translation:

A youthful shepherd, wandering and feeling
far from his heart's content, goes sad and lonely,
his thoughts on one he loves, and for her only
his breast pierced by love's wound, deep and unhealing.
He weeps not for the blows that love keeps dealing:
no, he has no regrets for the affliction
that tears him so: he weeps for his eviction
from her remembrance. How his heart is reeling . . .

St. John continues in this vein for two more stanzas, exhausting every bathetic trope of shepherd poetry dating back to the Greeks, and then he takes us aback by revealing the identity of his shepherd:

See him there where, at last, himself revealing
on a tree's branches, by fair arms extended,
he clings aloft, although his life has ended,
his breast pierced by love's wound, deep and
unhealing.

Here the translator, a mother of three sons, considers a boy's treatment at the treacherous hands of her own sex. I marvel that St. John could have written such a poem, and I submit that it could have only been translated so effectively by a watchful mother-in-law.

Peace be to the poet saints Terese and Francis. I yield to nobody in my regard for Thomas Aquinas' hymn *Tantum Ergo*. But I think you have to go back to King David to find devotional verse that rivals St. John's in its purity and power. And Rhina Espaillat has lovingly crafted them in translations that are both true and beautiful.

—Timothy Murphy

A Word from the Translator about Saint John of the Cross
(Spain, 1542–1591)

If you are encountering the work of Saint John—or, as he is known in the Spanish-speaking world, San Juan de la Cruz—for the first time, you may be in for a surprise, especially if the phrase "religious poetry" suggests, in your experience, the church hymns we know and love and think of as a form of prayer. The lyrics of hymns are, of course, religious poetry, but only one variety, and one very different from what is produced by poets known as mystics, who often have a relationship to the deity that is more passionate than ordinary prayer, more intimate in its language, and often, during a first reading, almost shocking in the highly visual imagery with which they address God, and assume the role, not of the simple believer beseeching God for some favor, asking His forgiveness for some wrongdoing, or thanking Him for His gifts.

The mystic poets adopt very different roles in their verbal exchanges with or about God, and invent—as literature does in plays, novels, stories and dramatic poems—events, relationships and scenes that express passion toward God of an almost erotic nature. Sometimes the mystic poet imagines himself—his soul, that is—as the wife of God who has lost sight of Him and is seeking Him desperately in a world that he cannot endure without the one Beloved of every soul. The theme is the need for the living presence of God, and the lengths to which the soul bereft of that company will go in order to find Him.

There are mystic poets in other languages as well: George Herbert, John Donne, and Gerard Manley Hopkins, among others, are English mystic poets, and much earlier there were Hebrew mystics whose poems still stir the soul of believers by approaching the deity in the language of lovers, thereby conveying the passion with which human men and women approach each other's material being.

These poems I have loved since childhood, having heard them recited by believers long before I was mature enough to understand them, but even then responding to the beauty of their language, are among the Spanish work I have had the honor and pleasure of translating into English, which has been my second language since the age of seven. I hope that you, reader, whether religious or not, will value these poems for their depth of feeling, their effort to communicate that depth as it fills with a love—a spiritual need—that is difficult to convey otherwise.

—Rhina P. Espaillat

La fonte que mana y corre

versos de San Juan de la Cruz

The Spring that Feeds the Torrent

Poems by Saint John of the Cross

Cántico espiritual

¿Adónde te escondiste,
Amado, y me dejaste con gemido?
Como el ciervo huiste
habiéndome herido;
salí tras ti clamando y eras ido.

Pastores, los que fueres
allá por las majadas al otero,
si por ventura vieres
aquel que yo más quiero,
decidle que adolezco, peno y muero.

Buscando mis amores
iré por esos montes y riberas;
no cogeré las flores,
ni temeré a las fieras,
y pasaré los fuertes y fronteras.

A Spiritual Canticle of the Soul and the Bridegroom Christ

Where have you fled and vanished,
Beloved, since you left me here to moan?
Deer-like you leaped; then, banished
and wounded by my own,
I followed you with cries, but you had flown.

Shepherds, if you discover,
going about this knoll to tend your sheep,
the dwelling of that lover
whose memory I keep,
tell him I sicken unto death and weep.

To seek him, I shall scour
these trackless woods to where the rivers flow—
not stop to pick a flower,
not run from beasts—but go
past every fort and border that I know.

¡Oh bosques y espesuras
plantadas por la mano del Amado!,
¡oh prado de verduras
de flores esmaltado!,
decid si por vosotros ha pasado.

Mil gracias derramando
pasó por estos sotos con presura;
y, yéndolos mirando,
con sola su figura
vestidos los dejó de su hermosura.

¡Ay!, ¿quién podrá sanarme?
Acaba de entregarte ya de veras;
no quieras enviarme
de hoy más mensajero
que no saben decirme lo que quiero.

Y todos cuantos vagan
de ti me van mil gracias refiriendo,
y todos más me llagan,
y déjanme muriendo
un no sé qué que quedan balbuciendo.

O forests darkly glooming,
seeded by my beloved's very hand!
O pasture richly blooming,
you flower-jeweled band!
I beg you, say if he has crossed your land.

Yes, with his thousand graces
streaming from him, he crossed these groves with speed,
and, glancing at these places—
with no more word or deed—
left them in his own beauty liveried.

Alas, who can content me?
Give yourself up to me, at last, entire;
nor send, as you have sent me,
those messengers you hire
who cannot tell me all that I desire.

And those who pass make clamor,
your thousand graces to my ear relaying,
wound me with words they stammer,
and kill me, ill-conveying
the who-knows-what that baffles all their saying.

Mas, ¿cómo perseveras,
¡oh vida!, no viendo donde vives,
y hacienda por que mueras
las flechas que recibes
de lo que del Amado en ti concibes?

¿Por qué, pues has llagado
aqueste corazón, no le sanaste?
Y, pues me le has robado,
¿por qué así le dejaste,
y no tomas el robo que robaste?

Apaga mis enojos,
pues que ninguno basta a deshacerlos,
y véante mis ojos,
pues eres lumbre de ellos,
y sólo para ti quiero tenerlos.

Descubre tu presencia,
y máteme tu vista y hermosura;
mira que la dolencia
de amor, que no se cura
sino con la presencia y la figura.

But how do you persever,
O life! in life not living, as you do,
pursued to death forever
by arrows that strike true,
aimed by that love the lover sows in you?

And why, having arrived
home to my heart, not heal it with relieving?
Why, since you have deprived
me of it, leave it grieving,
rather than grasp the plunder of your thieving?

Extinguish all my plight,
since there is none but you alone to do it;
Be present to my sight,
Since you alone renew it,
and you alone, when seen, give value to it.

Be present, drop your veil,
and let me die your beauty apprehending;
this grief that makes me pale
with love, can have no ending
without your presence, every joy transcending.

¡Oh cristalina fuente,
si en esos tus semblantes plateados
formases de repente
los ojos deseados
que tengo en mis entrañas dibujados!

¡Apártalos, Amado,
que voy de vuelo!
Vuélvete, paloma,
que el ciervo vulnerado
par el otero asoma
al aire de tu vuelo, y fresco toma.

Mi Amado las montañas,
los valles solitarios nemorosos,
las ínsulas extrañas,
los ríos sonorosos,
el silbo de los aires amorosos,

la noche sosegada
en par de los levantes de la aurora,
la música callada,
la soledad sonora,
la cena que recrea y enamora.

O crystal fountain flowing,
if in your silver stream I might discern
them there, suddenly glowing—
those eyes that make me burn,
deep in my heart inscribed—for which I yearn!

Turn them, Beloved, from me,
or I must fly to find you!
Turn, my dove,
love's wound has overcome me;
Deer-like, I stand above,
cooled by the breezes stirred by wings of love.

My lover is the highlands,
he is the wooded valleys lone and deep,
the far, mysterious islands,
the streams that sing and leap,
whispering winds that court the fields they sweep,

the night whose stillness pleases
and ushers morning and the rising sun,
silence whose music eases,
music from silence spun,
and supper that delights when day is done.

Cogednos las raposas,
que está ya florecida nuestra viña
en tanto que de rosas
hacemos una piña,
y no aparezca nadie en la campiña.

Detente, cierzo muerto;
ven, astro, que recuerdas los amores,
aspira por mi huerto,
y corran tus olores,
y pacerá el Amado entre las flores.

¡Oh ninfas de Judea!,
en tanto que en las flores y rosales
el ámbar perfumea,
poblad los arrabales,
y no queráis tocar nuestros umbrales.

Escóndete, Carillo,
y mira con tu faz a las montañas,
y no quieras decirlo;
mas mira las campañas
de la que va por ínsulas extrañas.

Hunt the quick foxes finding
our vineyard, where the tender shoots abound,
while we make garlands, binding
the stems of roses round,
and let no man be seen on the high ground.

Halt, you North wind, death-maker;
now come, wind from the South, by love beguiled,
breathe on my flowered acre,
spreading your fragrance mild,
and my Lover shall graze where blooms grow wild.

O, you Judean maidens!
Now that the rosetrees and the garden's flowers
with rich perfume are laden,
keep to your distant bowers
and do not tread these thresholds that are ours.

My dear one, hide, take shelter,
turn your face to the hills that stand in rows,
and speak not; see the welter
of maids about her where she goes,
wandering the strange islands no one knows.

A las aves ligeras,
leones, ciervos, gamos saltadores,
montes, valles, riberas,
aguas, aires, ardores,
y miedos de las noches veladores:

Por las amenas liras
y canto de sirenas os conjuro
que cesen vuestras iras
y no toquéis al muro,
porque la esposa duerma más seguro.

Entrado se ha la esposa
en el ameno huerto deseado,
y a su sabor reposa,
el cuello reclinado
sobre los dulces brazos del Amado.

Debajo del manzano,
allí conmigo fuiste desposada;
allí te di la mano,
y fuiste reparada
donde tu madre fuera violada.

Birds who fly hither lightly,
you lions, fawns and leaping fallow deer,
woods, vales, and rivers sprightly,
winds, waters, heats that sear,
and terrors that surround the night with fear:

By lyres and their soft sighing
I do beseech you, by the sirens' song:
silence your angry crying,
halt where the walls rise strong,
to keep the sleeping bride secure from wrong.

The bride has come to rest in
the pleasant garden's most alluring space,
and at her ease to nest in
her quiet leaning place,
within the sweetness of the groom's embrace.

Under the apple boughs,
there did I take you when our troth was plighted,
there gave my hand and vows,
and there you were requited,
where once your mother was abased and slighted.

Nuestro lecho florido,
de cueva de leones enlazado,
en púrpura teñido,
de paz edificado,
de mil escudos de oro coronado.

A zaga de tu huella
las jóvenes recorren el camino,
al toque de centella,
al adobado vino,
emisiones de bálsamo divino.

En la interior bodega
de mi Amado bebí, y, cuando salía
por toda aquesta vega,
ya cosa no sabía,
y el ganado perdí que antes seguía.

Allí me dio su pecho,
allí me enseñó ciencia muy sabrosa,
y yo le di de hecho
a mí, sin dejar cosa;
allí le prometí de ser su esposa.

Our marriage-couch, made festive
with flowers, with lion's grottoes posted round,
all purple-hung, suggestive
of peace within it bound,
and with a thousand golden emblems crowned.

There where your steps precede them,
the maidens follow in an eager line
where torches lead them,
and the spiced wine,
and the balsamic scent of the divine.

In my Beloved's cellar
I drank, and after tasting from his store,
wandered those fields, a dweller
in bliss, and cared no more
for the lost flocks that were my care before.

There at his breast he fed me,
there taught me knowledge sweet, with pleasure rife;
there where he led me
I gave myself for life
entirely, and pledged to be his wife.

Mi alma se ha empleado,
y todo mi caudal, en su servicio;
ya no guardo ganado,
ni ya tengo otro oficio,
que ya sólo en amar es mi ejercicio.

Pues ya si en el ejido
de hoy más no fuere vista ni hallada,
diréis que me he perdido,
que, andando enamorada,
me hice perdediza y fui ganada.

De flores y esmeraldas,
en las frescas mañanas escogidas,
haremos las guirnaldas,
en tu amor florecidas
y en un cabello mío entretejidas.

En sólo aquel cabello
que en mi cuello volar consideraste,
mirástele en mi cuello
y en él preso quedaste,
y en uno de mis ojo te llagaste.

My soul, in his employment,
spends all its wealth, forsakes its own affairs;
no flocks provide enjoyment,
no task, but that which bears
on love alone, and on no other cares.

If, where the flocks are feeding,
from this day forth I am no longer found,
say Love is leading
me a dizzy round,
and I have let myself be lost—and bound.

We shall weave emeralds, flowers
picked when the earliest rays of morning shine,
garlands grown by the powers
of your own love, to twine
about a single strand, a hair of mine.

One hair you chanced to note,
about my neck, that did your glance awaken.
You glimpsed it at my throat,
were snared and shaken,
and wounded by my eye and wholly taken.

Cuando tú me mirabas,
su gracia en mí tus ojos imprimían;
por eso me adamabas,
y en eso merecían
los míos adorar lo que veían.

No quieras despreciarme,
que si color moreno en mí hallaste,
ya bien puedes mirarme,
después que me miraste,
que gracia y hermosura en mí dejaste.

La blanca palomica
al arca con el ramo se ha tornado,
y ya la tortolica
al socio deseado
en las verdes riberas ha hallado.

En soledad vivía,
y en soledad ha puesto ya su nido,
y en soledad la guía
a solas su querido,
también en soledad de amor herido.

Whenever you beheld me,
your eyes imprinted all their graces there,
mastered and quelled me;
and my eyes earned their share:
to worship all in you that sight laid bare.

Do not, I beg, despise
the swarthy skin in which your sight first knew me;
look on me now: your eyes
have scattered through me
the beauty of the gaze with which you drew me.

That snowy little dove
bearing the branch back to the ark is flying—
the turtle, high above—
happily spying
on the green banks the Love for which she's sighing.

She once lived lonely,
and now, alone, has settled in her nest,
guided alone and only
by One she loves the best,
who, wounded for love's sake, has come to rest.

Gócemonos, Amado,
y vámonos a ver en tu hermosura
al monte y al collado,
do mana el agua pura;
entremos más adentro en la espesura.

Y luego a las subidas
cavernas de la piedra nos iremos
que están bien escondidas,
y allí nos entraremos,
y el mosto de granadas gustaremos.

Allí me mostrarías
aquello que mi alma pretendía,
y luego me darías
allí tú, vida mía,
aquello que me diste el otro día.

El aspirar el aire,
el canto de la dulce filomena,
el soto y su donaire
en la noche serena,
con llama que consume y no da pena.

Let us find joy together,
Beloved, in your beauty find our looks
reflected, whether
on hills or in pure brooks;
let us go deep into those wooded nooks.

Then to high, hidden
crevices in stony desert waste—
caves none can find unbidden—
we'll go, untraced,
where pomegranate wine is ours to taste.

You would delight me, showing
me, there, those things my spirit yearns to know,
and later by bestowing,
O Love I treasure so!
what first you gave to me some days ago.

Air, in its even breathing;
the song sweet Philomel sings in her flight;
the grove, its peace bequeathing
to gentle night,
with flames consuming all in painless light.

Que nadie lo miraba,
Aminadab tampoco aparecía
y el cerco sosegaba,
y la caballería
a vista de las aguas descendía.

And none to apprehend it;
Aminadab quite gone, without a trace;
the siege quietly ended,
horsemen halting their race,
dismounting near the waters of that place.

Glosa: Sin arrimo y con arrimo

Sin arrimo y con arrimo,
sin luz y a oscuras viviendo
todo me voy consumiendo.

Mi alma está desasida
de toda cosa criada
y sobre sí levantada
y en una sabrosa vida
sólo en su Dios arrimada.

Por eso ya se dirá
la cosa que más estimo
que mi alma se ve ya
sin arrimo y con arrimo.

Glosa: Apart and Not Yet a Part

Apart and not yet a part,
I live lightless and unseeing
to be consumed out of being.

My soul hungers for release
from all earthly things created,
and above itself elated
would live in delightful peace,
all but God repudiated.

Let them say it, as they may—
most joyful news to my heart—
that my soul has turned away,
apart and not yet a part.

Y aunque tinieblas padezco
en esta vida mortal
no es tan crecido mi mal
porque si de luz carezco
tengo vida celestial
porque el amor da tal vida
cuando más ciego va siendo
que tiene al ama rendida
sin luz y a oscuras viviendo.

Hace tal obra el amor
después que le conocí
que si hay bien o mal en mí
todo lo hace de un sabor
y al alma transforma en sí
y así en su llama sabrosa
la cual en mí estoy sintiendo
apriesa sin quedar cosa,
todo me voy consumiendo.

Although mist obscures my sight,
mortality seems nocturnal
darkness, but not infernal,
since, although I lack for light,
I've been given life eternal:
the love of a life so prized—
blind love, toward its object fleeing—
keeps my soul so mesmerized
I live lightless and unseeing.

For love such wonders has wrought—
since our friendship came to be—
that good and evil in me
have his flavor, leaving naught
in my soul that is not he,
so that his flame, as it travels
through me, gladly rushes, freeing
all that it finds, which unravels
to be consumed out of being.

Glosa a lo divino

Por toda la hermosura
nunca yo me perderé,
sino por un no sé qué
que se alcança por ventura.

I

Sabor de bien que es finito
lo más que puede llegar
es cansar el apetito
y estragar el paladar
y assí por toda dulçura
nunca yo me perderé
sino por un no sé qué
que se halla por ventura.

Glosa to the Divine

The beauty that can be eyed
will never be my undoing,
but rather what, beyond viewing,
only fortune can provide.

I

The taste of what can't endure
does no more, when it's diminished
desire, than make impure
the palate, whose joys are finished;
sweets whose sweet cannot abide
will never be my undoing,
but rather what, beyond viewing,
only fortune can provide.

II

El coraçon generoso
nunca cura de parar
donde se puede passar
sino en más difficultoso
nada le causa hartura
y sube tanto su fee
que gusta de un no sé qué
que se halla por ventura.

III

El que de amor adolesce
de el divino ser tocado
tiene el gusto tan trocado
que a los gustos desfallece
como el que con calentura
fastidia el manjar que ve
y apetece un no sé qué
que se halla por ventura.

II

A generous heart disdains
to loiter where travel's restful:
it prefers to take the stressful
route, where, beset by pains,
it will not be turned aside
from its undeterred pursuing
of what it knows, without viewing,
only fortune can provide.

III

He who knows the pain of love
by the divine hand ignited
finds himself no more delighted
by tastes he has wearied of,
as the sick man, satisfied
with no mess of potage stewing,
hungers for what, beyond viewing,
only fortune can provide.

IV

No os maravilléis de aquesto
que el gusto se queda tal
porque es la causa del mal
ajena de todo el resto
y assí toda criatura
enajenada se vee
y gusta de un no sé qué
que se halla por ventura.

V

Que estando la voluntad
de divinidad tocada
no puede quedar pagada
sino con divinidad
más, por ser tal su hermosura
que solo se vee por fee,
gústala en un no sé qué
que se halla por ventura.

IV

Do not find it strange to learn
such a taste can so persever
so unlike all else whatever
is the food for which you yearn
that all creatures far and wide
are torn from themselves with ruing
the lack of what, beyond viewing,
only fortune can provide.

V

For if once the will has known
the touch of the true divine,
for nothing less can it pine
than divinity alone.
Such beauty cannot be spied
but by faith itself, close hewing
to delights that, beyond viewing,
only fortune can provide.

VI

Pues, de tal enamorado
dezidme si abréis dolor
pues que no tiene sabor
entre todo lo criado
solo sin forma y figura
sin hallar arrimo y pie
gustando allá un no sé qué
que se halla por ventura.

VII

No penséis que el interior
que es de mucha más valía
halla gozo y alegría
en lo que acá de sabor
mas sobre toda hermosura
y lo que es y será y fue
gusta de allá un no sé qué
que se halla por ventura.

VI

Tell me, then, how such a lover
should not give you grief to bear,
since no substance does he wear—
no form or feature for cover—
of all who on earth reside,
kinship and support eschewing,
seeking for what, beyond viewing,
only fortune can provide.

VII

Do not believe that the core,
whose value is so much higher,
finds the joy that lights desire
in what here we hunger for:
present beauty—and, beside,
past and future, all accruing—
is less than what, beyond viewing,
only fortune can provide.

VIII

Más emplea su cuydado
quien se quiere aventajar
en lo que está por ganar
que en lo que tiene ganado
y assí, para más altura
yo siempre me inclinaré
sobre todo a un no sé qué
que se halla por ventura.

IX

Por lo que por el sentido
puede acá comprehenderse
y todo lo que entenderse
aunque sea muy subido
ni por gracia y hermosura
yo nunca me perderé
sino por un no sé qué
que se halla por ventura.

VIII

Better does he swell his hoard
who labors for future reaping,
than one more busy with heaping
harvest he has lately stored.
Therefore to be magnified
I am ever up and doing,
to gain the prize beyond viewing
only fortune can provide.

IX

Which is why I take my stand
that what our senses perceive
as beauty—though we believe
it fair and pronounce it grand—
the beauty that can be eyed
will never be my undoing,
but rather what, beyond viewing,
only fortune can provide.

Entréme donde no supe: Coplas

Entréme donde no supe
y quedéme no sabiendo
toda ciencia trascendiendo.

Yo no supe dónde entraba
pero cuando allí me vi
sin saber dónde me estaba
grandes cosas entendí
no diré lo que sentí
que me quedé no sabiendo
toda ciencia trascendiendo.

De paz y de piedad
era la ciencia perfecta,
en profunda soledad
entendida vía recta
era cosa tan secreta
que me quedé balbuciendo
toda ciencia trascendiendo.

I Went In, I Knew Not Where

I went in, I knew not where
and stayed, not knowing, but going
past the boundaries of knowing.

I knew not the place around me,
how I came there or where from,
but seeing where then I found me,
I sensed great things, and grew dumb—
since no words for them would come—
lacking all knowledge, but going
past the boundaries of knowing.

Of piety and of peace
I had perfect comprehension;
solitude without surcease
showed the straight way, whose intention—
too secret for me to mention—
left me stammering, but going
past the boundaries of knowing.

Estaba tan embebido
tan absorto y ajenado
que se quedó mi sentido
de todo sentir privado
y el espíritu dotado
de un entender no entendiendo
toda ciencia trascendiendo.

El que allí llega de vero
de sí mismo desfallece
cuanto sabía primero
mucho bajo le parece
y su ciencia tanto crece
que se queda no sabiendo,
toda ciencia trascendiendo.

Cuanto más alto se sube
tanto menos se entendía
que es la tenebrosa nube
que a la noche esclarecía
por eso quien la sabía
queda siempre no sabiendo,
toda ciencia trascendiendo.

So wholly rapt, so astonished
was I, from myself divided,
that my very senses vanished
and left me there unprovided
with knowledge, my spirit guided
by learning unlearned, and going
past the boundaries of knowing.

He who reaches that place truly
wills himself from self to perish;
all he lately knew, seen newly,
seems trifles unfit to cherish;
his new knowledge grows to flourish
so that he lingers there, going
past the boundaries of knowing.

The higher up one is lifted,
the less one perceives by sight
how the darkest cloud has drifted
to elucidate the night;
He who knows the dark aright
endures forever, by going
past the boundaries of knowing.

Este saber no sabiendo
es de tan alto poder
que los sabios arguyendo
jamás le pueden vencer
que no llega su saber
a no entender entendiendo
toda ciencia trascendiendo.

Y es de tan alta excelencia
aqueste sumo saber
que no hay facultad ni ciencia
que le puedan emprender
quien se supiere vencer
con un no saber sabiendo,
toda ciencia trascendiendo.

Y si lo queréis oír
consiste esta suma ciencia
en un subido sentir
de la divinal esencia
es obra de su clemencia
hacer quedar no entendiendo
todo ciencia trascendiendo.

This wisdom, wise by unknowing,
wields a power so complete
that the learnèd wise men throwing
wisdom against it compete
with a force none can defeat,
since their wisdom makes no showing
past the boundaries of knowing.

There is virtue so commanding
in this high knowledge that wit,
human skill and understanding
cannot hope to rival it
in one who knows how to pit
against self his selfless going
past the boundaries of knowing.

And if you should care to learn
what this mode of being wise is,
it is yearnings that discern
the Divine in all its guises,
whose merciful gift and prize is
to confound all knowledge, going
past the boundaries of knowing.

Letrillos

1. Navidad

Del Verbo divino
la Virgen preñada
viene de camino:
¡si le dais posada!

2. Suma de la perfección

Olvido de lo criado,
memoria del Criador,
atención a lo interior
y estarse amando al Amado.

Quatrains

1. Nativity

With God's Word—the burgeon
that swells in her womb—
now she comes, the Virgin:
if you give her room!

2. The Sum of Perfection

Forget created things,
but their Creator, never;
the core attend forever;
love Him from whom love springs.

Cantar de la alma que se huelga de conoscer a Dios por fee

¡Qué bien sé yo la fonte que mana y corre,
aunque es de noche!

I

Aquella eterna fonte está escondida.
¡Qué bien sé yo do tiene su manida
aunque es de noche!

II

Su origen no lo sé pues no le tiene
mas sé que todo origen della viene
aunque es de noche.

III

Sé que no puede ser cosa tan bella,
y que cielos y tierra beben della
aunque es de noche.

Song of the Soul that Takes Pleasure in Knowing God by Faith

How well I know the spring that feeds the torrent,
though night has fallen!

I

The spring runs from forever, and past finding;
how well I know it as it flows down winding,
though night has fallen.

II

Since it has none, I know not where its source is,
but know that there all things begin their courses,
though night has fallen.

III

I know nowhere exists so fair a treasure,
yet heaven and earth there slake their thirst with pleasure,
though night has fallen.

IV

Bien sé que suelo en ella no se halla
y que ninguno puede vadealla
aunque es de noche.

V

Su claridad nunca es escurecida
y sé que toda luz de ella es venida
aunque es de noche.

VI

Sé ser tan caudalosos sus corrientes,
que infiernos cielos riegan y a las gentes
aunque es de noche.

VII

El corriente que nace desta fuente
bien sé que es tan capaz y omnipotente
aunque es de noche.

VIII

El corriente que de estas dos procede
sé que ninguna de ellas le precede
aunque es de noche.

IV

I know it has no bottom to be found
and none can ford its waters and touch ground,
though night has fallen.

V

So clear it shines that nothing foul can scum it,
and every light, I know, emanates from it,
though night has fallen.

VI

So full its current, and so strongly churning,
that heaven rains on hell and on the burning,
though night has fallen.

VII

The stream that flows, I know, from that first welling
equals the source in might beyond all telling,
though night has fallen.

VIII

The stream that from these two flows forth together
keeps equal pace, as bonded by a tether,
though night has fallen.

IX

Aquesta eterna fonte está escondida
en este vivo pan por darnos vida
aunque es de noche.

X

Aquí se está llamando las criaturas
y de esta agua se hartan, aunque a escuras
porque es de noche.

XI

Aquesta viva fuente que deseo
en este pan de vida yo la veo
aunque es de noche.

IX

For that eternal spring is safely hidden
in this, life's bread, the feast to which we're bidden,
though night has fallen.

X

They're called to this, all creatures here abiding,
to come and drink their fill, although in hiding,
since night has fallen.

XI

That living fountain that I most desire
I find in this, the bread of life, entire,
though night has fallen.

Canciones de el alma en la íntima comunicación de unión de amor de Díos

¡Oh llama de amor viva,
que tiernamente hieres
de mi alma en el más profundo centro!
pues ya no eres esquiva,
acaba ya si quieres;
rompe la tela de este dulce encuentro.

¡Oh cauterio suave!
¡Oh regalada llaga!
¡Oh mano blanda! ¡Oh toque delicado,
que a vida eterna sabe
y toda deuda paga!,
matando muerte en vida la has trocado.

¡Oh lámparas de fuego
en cuyos resplandores
las profundas cavernas del sentido
que estaba oscuro y ciego
con extraños primores
calor y luz dan junto a su querido!

Songs of the Soul in Intimate Amorous Communion with God

O love, you living flame
who wound with tender fire
my very soul, down to its depths descending!
No longer hushed by shame,
come now, to your desire;
sunder the veil that parts for sweet befriending.

O soft subjection!
O wound that joys beget!
O gentle hand! O touch with pleasures rife
that hints at resurrection
and ransoms every debt!
You have done death to death, and made it life.

O fiery lamps ignited—
whose bright resplendent gleams
light those deep caverns where the mind, in hiding,
dwelt blind and all benighted—
your dazzling radiance streams
warm rays on the beloved there abiding!

¡Cuán manso y amoroso
recuerdas en mi seno
donde secretamente solo moras
y en tu aspirar sabroso
de bien y gloria lleno
cuán delicadamente me enamoras!

How tenderly you love me
and conjure in my breast—
that secret place where you alone are treasured—
how—your sweet breath above me—
by heaven's good possessed—
with what rare lover's skill have I been pleasured!

Coplas: Tras de un amoroso lance

Tras de un amoroso lance
y no de esperanza falto
volé tan alto tan alto
que le di a la caza alcance.

Para que yo alcance diese
a aqueste lance divino
tanto volar me convino
que de vista me perdiese
y con todo en este trance
en el vuelo quedé falto
mas el amor fue tan alto
que le di a la caza alcance.

Cuanto más alto llegaba
de este lance tan subido
tanto más bajo y rendido
y abatido me hallaba
dije: "No habrá quien alcance".
Abatíme tanto tanto
que fui tan alto tan alto
que le di a la caza alcance.

Coplas: In Pursuit

In pursuit of amatory
adventure, hope bid me fly
and I rose so high, so high
that I closed upon the quarry.

To achieve so great a height,
divine adventure pursuing,
I flew so far that the doing
lifted me clear beyond sight.
A flight so extraordinary
rendered me too faint to fly:
It was love drew me so high
that I closed upon the quarry.

As I rose up high and higher—
my divine prey still uncaught—
weary and heartsick, I thought,
fallen from my one desire,
"All such attempts must miscarry."
So cast down by this was I
that I rose up high, up high,
until I closed on the quarry.

Por una extraña manera
mil vuelos pasé de un vuelo
porque esperanza del cielo
tanto alcanza cuanto espera
esperé solo este lance
y en esperar no fui falto
pues fui tan alto tan alto,
que le di a la caza alcance.

Somehow I contrived to go
a thousandfold by once reaching:
heaven grants to the beseeching
what they earn through hope. For no
prize but this prey would I tarry,
and hope raised me by and by,
until I was high, so high
that I closed upon the quarry.

El pastorcico

Un pastorcico solo está penando
Ajeno de placer y de contento
Y en su pastora puesto el pensamiento
Y el pecho del amor muy lastimado.

No llora por haberle amor llagado
Que no le pena verse así afligido
Aunque en el corazón está herido
Mas llora por pensar que está olvidado.

Que sólo de pensar que está olvidado
De su bella pastora con gran pena
Se deja maltratar en tierra ajena
El pecho del amor muy lastimado.

Y dice el pastorcico: "¡Ay desdichado
De aquel que de mi amor ha hecho ausencia
Y no quiere gozar la mi presencia
Y el pecho por su amor muy lastimado!"

The Youthful Shepherd

A youthful shepherd, wandering and feeling
far from his heart's content, goes sad and lonely,
his thoughts on one he loves, and for her only
his breast pierced by love's wound, deep and unhealing.

He weeps—not for the blows that love keeps dealing—
no, he has no regrets for the affliction
that tears him so: he weeps for his eviction
from her remembrance. How his heart is reeling

to know that she forgets him who is kneeling
before her! Just to think she has refused him
sends him afar, where strangers have abused him,
his breast pierced by love's wound, deep and unhealing.

He cries, "Unlucky she, forever steeling
herself against my love, she who retires
when I approach, frustrating my desires,
my breast pierced by love's wound, deep and unhealing!"

Y al cabo de un gran rato se ha encumbrado
Sobre un árbol do abrió sus brazos bellos
Y muerto se ha quedado asido de ellos
Del pecho del amor muy lastimado.

See him there where, at last, himself revealing
on a tree's branches, by fair arms extended
he clings aloft, although his life has ended,
his breast pierced by love's wound, deep and unhealing.

Coplas del alma que pena por ver a Dios

Vivo sin vivir en mí
y de tal manera espero
que muero porque no muero.

I

En mí yo no vivo ya
y sin dios vivir no puedo
pues sin él y sin mí quedo
¿este vivir qué será?
Mil muertes se me hará
pues mi misma vida espero
muriendo porque no muero.

II

Esta vida que yo vivo
es privación de vivir
y assí es continuo morir
hasta que viva contigo.
Oye mi Dios lo que digo
que esta vida no la quiero
que muero porque no muero.

Verses of the Soul that Pines to See God

Not in myself do I live
but in such great hope, that I
die of my longing to die.

I

I no longer live in me;
lacking God, from life I'm driven;
lacking God or self to live in,
what, then, can this living be?
A thousand deaths is the fee,
since life must come, by and by,
and I die, longing to die.

II

This life that I now endure
is not life but its denial;
a continuous death, my trial
till I dwell with you secure.
Gather, my Lord, with what sure
contempt from this life I fly
and I die, longing to die.

III

Estando ausente de tí
qué vida puedo tener
sino muerte padecer
la mayor que nunca vi?
Lástima tengo de mí
pues de suerte persevero
que muero porque no muero.

IV

El pez que del agua sale
aun de alibio no carece
que en la muerte que padesce
al fin la muerte le vale.
Qué muerte abrá que se yguale
a mi vivir lastimero
pues si más vivo más muero?

V

Quando me pienso alibiar
de verte en el Sacramento
házeme más sentimiento
el no te poder gozar
todo es para más penar
por no verte como quiero
y muero porque no muero.

III

Absent, as I am, from you,
what life can I have but death
who suffer, in drawing breath,
what the worst of deaths can do?
I regard my fate with rue;
my misfortunes multiply;
I die of longing to die.

IV

The fish that's pulled from the wave
finds balm of a certain sort:
the death he suffers is short
and brings the rest he may crave.
But what death could be as grave
as mine, who in life must sigh,
and live more, the more to die?

V

What comfort I taste is brief
finding you in bread and wine:
to know you cannot be mine
recalls me to greater grief.
I sorrow without relief
for the sight that you deny,
and die, for I long to die.

VI

Y si me gozo Señor
con esperança de verte
en ver que puedo perderte
se me dobla mi dolor
viviendo en tanto pabor
y esperando como espero
muérome porque no muero.

VII

Sácame de aquesta muerte
mi Dios y dame la vida
no me tengas impedida
en este lazo tan fuerte
mira que peno por verte,
y mi mal es tan entero
que muero porque no muero.

VIII

Lloraré mi muerte ya
y lamentaré mi vida
en tanto que detenida
por mis pecados está.
¡O mi Dios! quanta será
quando yo diga vero
vivo ya porque no muero?

VI

My joy, Lord, is to believe
that I shall behold you clear;
but doubting you will appear
causes me doubly to grieve
when such terror I conceive,
harboring a hope so high,
that I die, longing to die.

VII

From this my death set me free,
my God, to the life I crave;
do not bind me like a slave
in these bonds that hinder me.
Look how I languish to see
you, my God, and how I sigh,
and die of longing to die.

VIII

I shall mourn my death away
and weep for my life to come,
while my sins detain me from
the new for which I pray.
I, my God! When shall I say—
and say truthfully—that I
live, and no longer die?

En una noche oscura: Canción de la subida del Monte Carmel

En una noche oscura
con ansias en amores inflamada
¡oh dichosa ventura!
salí sin ser notada
estando ya mi casa sosegada,

a oscuras y segura
por la secreta escala disfrazada,
¡oh dichosa ventura!
a oscuras y en celada
estando ya mi casa sosegada.

En la noche dichosa
en secreto que nadie me veía
ni yo miraba cosa
sin otra luz y guía
sino la que en el corazón ardía.

Aquesta me guiaba
más cierto que la luz del mediodía
adonde me esperaba
quien yo bien me sabía
en sitio donde nadie aparecía.

The Dark Night of the Soul

One darkest night I went,
aflame with love's devouring eager burning—
O delirious event!—
no witnesses discerning,
the house now still from which my steps were turning.

Hidden by darkness, bent
on flight, disguised, down secret steps sojourning—
O delirious event!—
Hidden by dark, and yearning,
the house now still from which my steps were turning;

In that most blissful night,
in secrecy, since none had seen my going,
nor did I pause for sight,
nor had I light, for showing
the route, but that which in my heart was glowing.

This only did the guiding,
surer than the blaze when noonday shone,
to where he was abiding—
who was to me well known—
where we would be together and alone.

¡Oh noche, que guiaste!
¡Oh noche amable más que la alborada!
¡Oh noche que juntaste
amado con amada,
amada en el amado transformada!

En mi pecho florido,
que entero para él solo se guardaba
allí quedó dormido
y yo le regalaba
y el ventalle de cedros aire daba.

El aire de la almena
cuando yo sus cabellos esparcía
con su mano serena
y en mi cuello hería
y todos mis sentidos suspendía.

Quedéme y olvidéme
el rostro recliné sobre el amado;
cesó todo, y dejéme
dejando mi cuidado
entre las azucenas olvidado.

O night that led me true,
O night more fair than morning's earliest shining,
O night that wrought from two—
lover, beloved entwining—
beloved and lover one in their combining!

On my new-flowered breast,
to him alone and wholly sanctified,
he leaned and lay at rest;
his pleasure was my guide,
and cedars to the wind their scent supplied.

Down from the tower, breezes
came, while soft fingers winnowed through his hair;
a touch that wounds and pleases
caressed my throat with air,
leaving every sense suspended there.

I stayed, all else forgetting,
inclined toward the beloved, face to face;
all motion halted, letting
care vanish with no trace,
forgotten in the lilies of that place.

Acknowledgments

My earliest thanks for my encounter with this beloved author, as is so often the case with texts in my native language, must go to my mother and father, whose devotion to the written word—and most especially Spanish poetry—enriched my life since its beginnings.

But my gratitude for the translations that flowed from that encounter belongs to Dr. Joseph Bottum, who encouraged me out of my hesitation when he first suggested that I attempt what felt, at first, like sacrilege, and emboldened me to submit work to *First Things,* where these translations first appeared.

That labor of love led me to further, and equally daring, attempts at cross-translating poems I loved in both of my languages, thereby persuading my father that bilinguality would not entail the loss he feared—that of my native culture—but rather a gain of which he became very proud.

May translation continue to allow our species to share what we love, most especially each other.

—Rhina P. Espaillat

Versions of the following translations originally appeared in *First Things*:

"One Darkest Night" June/July 2003 and March 2010

"Verses of the Soul that Pines to See God" October 2003

"A Spiritual Canticle of the Soul and the Bridegroom of Christ" November 2003

"Song of the Soul that takes Pleasure in Knowing God by Faith" April 2006

"Songs of the Soul in Intimate Amorous Communion with God" August/September 2006

"Coplas: In Pursuit" December 2006

"I Went In, I knew Not Where" December 2006

"The Youthful Shepherd" March 2007

"Letrillos" March 2007

"Glosa: To the Divine" June/July 2007

"Glosa: Apart and Not Apart" June/July 2007

Versions of these poems appeared in *The Sewanee Theological Review* 56:1 (Christmas 2012)

The Spanish language originals of these poems are from:

The Penguin Book of Spanish Verse, ed. J.M Cohen (London and New York: Penguin, 1988)

www.los-poetas.com *Poesia: San Juan de la Cruz*, ed. Domingo Yndurán, Letreas Hispanicas No. 178 (Madrid: Ediciones Cátedra, 1997)

Poesias San Juan de la Cruz at www.mercaba.org/doctores/juan-cruz/poesias

About St. John of the Cross

San Juan de la Cruz (1542–1591), was born Juan de Yepez y Álavarez, in Fontiveros, Spain. While attending a boarding school for poor and orphaned children, he decided to pursue a religious vocation. In 1563, he entered the Carmelite Order. He was ordained in 1567 and considered joining the Carthusians, but after meeting St. Teresa of Ávila and witnessing her vision of deep contemplation, he set out to reform the corrupted Carmelite Order alongside her. Their efforts to return the Carmelites to the stricter, original rule eventually led to St. John's imprisonment. During this period, he endured tremendous suffering, including public lashings, isolation in a tiny cell, and a meager, penitential diet of bread and water, with occasional bits of salted fish. He was able to write poetry on scraps of paper smuggled in by the friar charged with guarding his cell. His poems draw on Italian and Hebrew verse, as well as Spanish folk songs. St. John is best known for his treatises, *Ascent of Mount Carmel* and *Dark Night,* in which he explains the meaning of his poetic masterpiece, "The Dark Night of the Soul." These commentaries chronicle the phases of purgation a soul must undergo in order to reach its final stage of mystical union with God. St. John of the Cross died of an infection on December 14, 1591 and was canonized by Benedict XIII in 1726.

About the Translator

Dominican-born Rhina P. Espaillat is a bilingual poet, essayist, short story writer, translator, and former English teacher in New York City's public high schools. She has published twelve books, five chapbooks, and a monograph on translation. She has earned numerous national and international awards, and is a founding member of the Fresh Meadows Poets of NYC and the Powow River Poets of Newburyport, MA. Her most recent works are three poetry collections: *And After All, The Field,* and *Brief Accident of Light: A Day in Newburyport,* co-authored with Alfred Nicol. Her numerous translations include work by Sor Juana Inés de la Cruz, San Juan de la Cruz, Garcia Lorca, Miguel Hernandez, Emily Dickinson, Walt Whitman, Robert Frost, Richard Wilbur, and many contemporary poets of the Americas and the Hispanic diaspora, among others.

Rhina P. Espaillat, dominicana de nacimiento y bilingue, es poeta, ensayista, cuentista y traductora, y fue por varios años maestra de inglés en las escuelas públicas secundarias de New York. Ha publicado doce libros, cinco libros de cordel, y un monógrafo sobre la traducción. Ha ganado varios premios nacionales e internacionales, y fue fundadora del grupo Fresh Meadows Poets en NYC y el grupo Powow River Poets en Newburyport. Sus obras más recientes son tres poemarios: *And After All, The Field,* y una collaboración con el poeta Alfred Nicol, *Brief Accident of Light: A Day in Newburyport.* Sus numerosas traducciones abarcan las obras de Sor Juana Inés de la Cruz, San Juan de la Cruz, García Lorca, Miguel Hernandez, Emily Dickinson, Walt Whitman, Robert Frost, Richard Wilbur, y muchos poetas contemporáneos de las Americas y la diáspora hispana, entre otros.

www.ingramcontent.com/pod-product-compliance
Lightning Source LLC
Chambersburg PA
CBHW050329120526
44592CB00014B/2117